Her Small Hands Were Not Beautiful

Maud Gonne in 1897 on a fundraising tour in the U.S.

Her Small Hands Were Not Beautiful

POEMS

BY

KATHRYN KIRKPATRICK

Copyright 2014 by Clemson University
ISBN 978-0-9890826-3-1

Published by Clemson University Press in Clemson, South Carolina

Editorial Assistants: Jessica Simpson and Charis Chapman

To order copies, please visit The Clemson University Press website: www.clemson.edu/press.

Contents

Acknowledgments • vi
Dedication • vii
Americans Breakfast at Bayview, Dublin • vii

☙

1. *Yeats Plays Golf* • 1
Crossing the Border • 2
In the Foul Rag-and-Bone-Shop of the Heart • 5
Canaire of Inis Cathaig • 7
Maud Gonne: First Meeting • 9
Woman of the Sidhe • 10
Undoubtedly Miss Edgeworth • 12
Multinational • 13
Villanelle for the Lost • 14
Yeats and the Gardener • 15
Yeats Plays Croquet • 16
Yeats Plays Golf • 17

2. *Maeve Married: A Sequence* • 19

**3. *"Her Small Hands Were Not Beautiful":
Voices in the Act of Remembering
Maud Gonne* • 29**

☙

Glossary • 62
A Note on the Author • 64

Acknowledgments

My thanks to the editors, readers, and staff of the following journals where these poems first appeared, sometimes in other versions:

"Woman of the Sidhe," *Kennesaw Review*; "Americans Breakfast at Bayview, Dublin," "Villanelle for the Lost," & "Canaire of Inis Cathaig," *Poem*; "Yeats and the Gardener," & "Yeats Plays golf," *The Recorder*; "Yeats Plays Croquet," *Kakalak: Anthology of Carolina Poets*; "Crossing the Border," *Southern Poetry Review*; "In the Foul Rag-and-Bone Shop of the Heart," "Undoubtedly Miss Edgeworth," "Maeve Married," & "Maud Gonne: First Meeting," *The South Carolina Review*.

"Americans Breakfast in Bayview, Dublin," "Maud Gonne: First Meeting," and "Crossing the Border" appeared in other versions in *Beyond Reason* (San Antonio: Pecan Grove Press, 2004); "Woman of the Sidhe" and "Undoubtedly Miss Edgeworth" appeared in *Out of the Garden* (Bay City, MI: Mayapple Press, 2007).

"Crossing the Border" was reprinted in *Don't Leave Hungry: Fifty Years of Southern Poetry Review*, James Smith, ed. (Fayetteville: University of Arkansas Press, 2009).

I am grateful to Appalachian State University for a Board of Trustees Travel Grant that allowed me to take up a writing residency at the Tyrone Guthrie Centre in Annaghmakerrig, Ireland; all of the Yeats poems were written there. My thanks as well to the Library of Congress for permission to use the photograph of Maud Gonne on her U.S. tour and to Dublin City Gallery The Hugh Lane for use of Sarah Purser's portrait of Gonne. Many of the photographs on the cover were made available by the Manuscript, Archives, and Rare Book Library of Emory University. A grant from Appalachian State's University Research Council allowed me to conduct research in these archives, where I discovered Conrad Balliet's interviews.

Without the masterful help of Molly Peacock, "Her Small Hands Were Not Beautiful" might never have seen the light of day. Conrad Balliet made that sequence possible by allowing me to make use of the brilliant interviews he conducted in the early 1970s. Wayne Chapman has for years been the kind of steadfast and generous editor every poet needs to sustain a writing life, while Susan Ludvigson has been my poetry touchstone over many years of friendship. Finally, without William Atkinson, who has kept the home-fires burning, I can hardly imagine any of it.

In memory of
my grandmother
Ruth Doherty Kirkpatrick
(1902–1991)

Americans Breakfast at Bayview, Dublin

When I come down
to serve them sausage and egg,
these women broad in jogging suits,
these men talking golf and directions,
they're already complaining
about the coffee, the traffic noise.

They puncture fresh tomatoes
and leave them on the plate,
discuss their children loudly.
The vegetarian son gone to Chile
will learn soon enough to eat meat.
They say *third world country*
like they say *burned toast*.

If I threw their ample bags
into Dublin Bay, archaeologists
ten thousand years on might find
crabs lodging in the plastic shells
of hair dryers, mollusks mirrored
in compacts, anemones smug
in leather running shoes.

There'd be no evidence then
of these Americans standing on shore,
will-less, the souls gone out of them.
Or of me, alone in the doorway,
wishing myself on an Inishmore cove,
my ancestors having dragged seaweed
across the rocky miles
to cultivate potatoes
with soil they handed up
between the stones.

1. Yeats Plays Golf

Crossing the Border

1

Behind the machine gun,
through the bullet-proof visor,
I might have met his eye,
from the rented car with Dublin plates,
from beside my English husband,
from the line of Ulster Protestants
I'd come from. Almost here,
this very ground.

Weaving through traffic in Derry
we'd somehow got between
two armored cars
with English soldiers hunched over guns.
And then those automatics
swiveled onto us.

I'd heard a Belfast woman
on call-in radio
say a soldier worried his trigger
whenever she hurried past. *Walk fast*
she'd been instructed. *Don't look at them.*
But something keeps me staring
into the leveled barrel.

2

We walk the streets of Derry
in the dusk, the fortressed inner city,
the shops on the town square
all barricaded by steel doors
against bomb blasts
and at the center, a monument
to soldiers in World Wars.
No mention of the fighting here.

In front of the Guild Hall
we stand, awkward beside
the cannon-riddled wall,
reading the town history, official,
and not so clear as words spray-painted
on the panopticon:

FAWK BIG BROTHER WHO'S WATCHING WHO?

    3

From Limavady and Coleraine,
from Castlebar and Ballymoney,
on and on they came,
the Protestant bands
in cobalt blue berets with orange plumes,
Men of Ulster, Pride of Ulster,
with their military faces,
their strange, unseeing stares,
a few accordions, some snares
but mostly marching men with flutes
and the drummer beating wildly.

They teach their young
the loud fierce beat, each band
with boys beside the striding
grown men, and one so young,
bewildered by the sound,
what did he hear as he stumbled
to keep time, almost trampled
in the turning?

In front of us, a young man
cheered, gave thumbs up
to the men he knew
and danced from street to curb,
punching the sky with his fist.
His lager glass rolled
into the street and tightlipped
a woman lifted it from among
the marching feet
onto the windowsill.

    4

Up the last ridge
to our Appalachian home
with the sky ripe and furred
as a peach. *Gloaming*. The word
in my ears like some tribal memory.
Here is where the Scots-Irish came

Her Small Hands Were Not Beautiful

three hundred years ago
from County Antrim and Tyrone,
rack-rented, then indentured,
stowed in the bowels of boats,
they came as we come now, weary but grateful
for this mountain-shouldered sky.

But the first night home
when I dream myself in red curls,
I pull them off to the black lengths
of a great-grandmother's hair.
Cherokee, from among these hills
driven to Oklahoma in tears?

I am that hybrid,
American, firing the shot
that pelts me. I am that other,
a woman, who always makes
her own country
furrow and brick
mortar and till.

In the Foul Rag-and-Bone Shop of the Heart
for Susan Ludvigson

In my own dream
I sat on a marble bench.
Above me, impossibly tall,
loomed Yeats, also in marble.
There were others, too,
possibly Eliot, but Yeats
is the one I remember.

Since then I've seen his statue
in Sligo. Yeats with insect legs,
winged, his poems inscribed
all over his body, a witty
and irreverent likeness,
the Irish sculptor correcting
my dream, bringing the poet
to scale.

You say I know him better
than you do, but my statues
are stony-eyed, not
a lift or kick in them.

The poem I open is "Prayer for my Daughter"
where I find the terms of the father's sanction
prayed over a sleeping child--
that she be like Lady Gregory
who gave him *Custom. Ceremony.*
The spreading laurel tree.
Whatever else, not like the public,
opinionated Maud

Old bellows full of angry wind.

The last time I saw my own father,
he was angry, his voice
thundering behind me as I left
the house. My leaving

was one of those choices
we make to keep living,
though the price was so heavy,

sometimes my knees still buckle,
breath caught in my chest.

I don't know what it means
to be sanctioned by fathers,
though once, at Thanksgiving,
my father dropped his warrior face
for days, we both did,
and in that fierce love
I felt immortal.

But as for your question,
I think the old wicked man
might have kicked any woman around.
Age burst in him like a boil,
Why should not old men be mad?
Having claimed the new poems
with his own mucky wildness,
he finally gave Gonne a reprieve.
Herself a statue in "A Bronze Head,"
human, superhuman, a bird's round eye,
he wondered who'd done her justice.

That's the most we'll get from him, I fear.
Kick, stony stare, or measured admission.
Is it my way of finding the father's sanction
to say that I believe this?
Whatever he said in the poems,
Maud was the one he loved best.

Canaire of Inis Cathaig

In the end
it must have made a difference
to her that she too could walk
on the water.

She had come from her hermitage
at nightfall, having said nocturns,
with only her staff
and the memory of a forest
without moonlight.

At the Shannon, ice choked
the current. Miles back
her own door stood open,
the coals of her fire
still glowed.

*Now let your servant depart
in peace*, and she entered
the river, water and ice
swarming her waist.
Nothing to guide her
but the dream of Senan's island.

How it happened even she
didn't know, but she leapt
from the crest of one wave

to another toward the island
where monks refused women
the bread and the wine.

And when he came down
to the harbor with his
women may not enter
she knew it was only
a matter of time.
She could stand there
for hours on the brink
of the water.

I am telling this story
because, once again,
it took a holy woman
performing miracles
to receive the sacrament
from an ordinary man.

Maud Gonne: First Meeting

She'd come out in her slippers,
kept a hansom cab waiting.

It was 1889. Bedford Park.
She rode all the way from Belgravia
to meet Jack Yeats and his son. Pushy man,
the father. But this poet
struggling to paint, she liked

his sad smile. *I make the cloak of Sorrow.*
Of course she said she loved his poems.
And that was the one thing he heard.
Like other men, he was frightened.
He hid his fingers stained with paint.

Years later she forgot the occasion
entirely, the leave-taking, and then
stepping out into Blenheim Road,
how the wind rose like a keen.
Dead leaves battened down her loose hair.

Instead, she remembered O'Leary
filling her arms with books —Thomas Davis,
Mangan and Ferguson—because she'd said
*I want to work for Ireland. I want you
to show me how.* Willie followed her home
from tea and they spoke of John's years
in Portland Jail breaking stones
after the Rising. In this way the poet
became confidante, friend. A character
in her own story.

Woman of the Sidhe

When you were younger
you seemed to care less
about being despised.

Men with porridge faces
damned the Land League
left tenants in ditches,
said, *Let them die*
These people must be taught
a lesson and you rose
from their tables, ordered
your carriage, turned
your back on the country house,
the hunt ball, the landlord's wife.

They hated you for your choice
not to be one of them, though
your face sometimes brought them
back, like moths to flame.

Sir John in Donegal dangled
wife like a diamond pendant
before you, *wife of a liberal MP.*
All afternoon, battering rams
at the doors of those cabins,
an old woman carried out
on a mattress, clutching a rosary,
another too weak to stand, her
day-old infant on the ground.
When he gave you the diamond
on its gold chain, you put it
in the hands of the farmer's wife,
rent for the year and more.

Arriving with your canaries and finches,
your Great Dane, Dagda, his paws in leather boots,
Woman of the Sidhe, the poor called you.
Soup Kitchens. Letters to the press.
You wanted to shelter everything fragile and torn.
New cottages in the countryside.
Cakes and porter and fiddlers to warm them.
But alone in each cramped hotel room,
sleeping upright to breath,

what you hid was the grey lady
in your dreams: *Murderess of children*
she called you, showed you the face
of your dead son.

Undoubtedly Miss Edgeworth

Yeats said that in your youth
you ran wild in Ireland:
cut out squares in a checked tablecloth,
trampled through the glass of hothouse frames
delighting in the crash.

Unfortunate genius he called you
because afterwards the boarding school
in Derby did its work so well,
taught you the arithmetic of fear:
your father especially, holed up in his study
or traveling by moonlight to talk botany,
marrying another young wife.

For Yeats you spoke just once in your work,
in your first book, your *great genius*,
that *natural talent for the unexpected*
lost in the daily rounds of daughter. Of duty.
Of all those novels written between four
in the afternoon and five.

*She could not persuade herself to trust
nature, to set down in tale and novel
the emotions and longings and chances.*
But for Yeats this was an abstract regret:
when the woman he himself loved
most in the world got up from tea in 1897
to continue the work she'd begun
(that day, to tend those the police had batoned
in the Jubilee Riot), he told them to lock
the door. He stood up in that club
in Rutland Square, demanding reasons,
explanations. He helped them to bar her way.

Multinational

At the shopping mall in Monaghan,
I could be anywhere. Not Ireland
any longer, but the artificial light
of the chain store, that quasi-familiar
nowhere, where like deranged fish,
we school toward the brand name
as if sating could happen here.

My Irish friend meets her husband
in McDonald's while I stroll
past everything I already know,
Hollywood movies out on DVD,
designer t-shirts, low-slung jeans.

I want to cry *turn back*.
Though for now it all looks benign,
the old streets still teeming with shop fronts,
the sidewalks alive with dailiness,
malls are like mint in the garden.
Turn your back and a sweet sameness
covers every other living thing.

Villanelle for the Lost

When the fish left its wake on the water
near the shady side of stones and brambles,
she thought of the net she had set in the river.

Under the green leaves of the lismore,
she reached for the net and stumbled
as the fish left a wake on the water.

A fine salmon is much like a lover
whose loss to the currents humbles.
Think of the net set in the river.

Though the table is empty, it's better
to refrain from the question that trembles
like the wake of a fish on the water.

Trembles and forces an answer:
What should I have done? What remembered?
Is grief like a net in a river?

Now she chooses the river for lover,
leaves the others their season of troubles.
When the fish leaves a wake on the water,
she thinks of the net once set in the river.

Yeats and the Gardener

The day Yeats died, the gardener died too.
They were buried at Rocquebrune side by side.

The poet's heart failed in the January cold.
Of the gardener we really know nothing.

Perhaps he pruned trees like overgrown poems,
cutting risky bargains with beauty.

Yeats died abroad without blood kin, no
sister or brother or daughter or son.

His wife and his lovers attended.
Of the gardener we really know nothing.

Perhaps his body sang toward loamy ground,
a turning he'd known through each winter.

After the war, when the Irish returned
some say they took the gardener for poet

carried his coffin to Drumcliff Churchyard
as instructed in "Under Ben Bulben."

Nine years into his death, did the poet
make a great change, his body revising

high and low, the roots of a tree
the gardener loved grown into his heart?

Perhaps when pilgrims travel to Yeats' grave,
they bend toward a French gardener's bones.

Yeats Plays Croquet

A tall man with a mallet must bend
to make contact at all, to send
the bright sphere through each hoop,
threading the careful lawn
like a rhyme stitches a stanza.

He made a serious game of it.
What chance did Norah McGuinnes have
when she came to tea and was chosen?

Cup suspended between saucer and chin,
her heart beat like Leda's
as the great man rose like a swan
in his white suit
and made for the field of play.

At first she felt her legs give way,
his voice a long way off,
her head muzzy.

But the sudden blow of wood on wood
brought her back in a white rush.
She aimed and swung and swung again
her body lighter with each hoop
until she saw his face, those fingers
pushing through his hair vaguely.

A strange shudder broke the afternoon
when they both saw she could best him.
What else could she do but loosen her grip,
each shot more askew than the last?
And what could he do, finally winning,
but put knowledge back on with power
and indifferently let her drop.

Yeats Plays Golf

A wild swing and he'd drop the club,
walk off in another direction,
head bowed, hands behind his back,
for all the world the great poet
working over a new line,
he and the ball he'd hit
having fallen out, parted company,
this time, perhaps, for good.

Smyllie and Duncan found them
in the furze bush, clambered
through ditches, performed
sleight of hand and the game
resumed, golf balls appearing
like fishes and loaves.

Is greatness the will to remake the world
in the image of desire?
He had written himself into nobility
so that the mere mention of taking up golf
produced young men in an MG,
a golf bag he called his quiver.
Smyllie, this is my quiver
and if he'd called the golf clubs
arrows, no one would have objected.
He was free to rename the world.

And aren't we?
           Shall we drop
what we're doing, retrieve
the odd ball, shoulder our quivers,
set off to ask the animals
their proper names, redraw
the boundaries of nations
so that contours of the land
dissolve the lines drawn on maps?
Believe me, I know what I'm asking.

When Yeats discovered the young men
sought to remake each green afternoon
in the image of his desire,
he produced a half-crown
from his pockets

for each golf ball surely lost,
keeping some account of the price
paid by others
for arranging the world as he wished.

2. Maeve Married
A Sequence

I demanded a strange bride-gift such as no woman before me had asked of a man....
—from "Táin Bó Cúailnge," Book of *Leinster*

Because she wanted a life
as filigreed with wonders
as any man's, they decided
she couldn't have loved him.

1

How to account for her?
Daughter of a High King?

Shall we give birth that privilege,
apply chromosome to gene
like a knife to a leek?

But accidents of birth solve nothing.
They are flame to a sharp stone.
Born a warrior or raised one,
she heard the usual complaints:

*I would never give in
to a woman, be under
a woman's rule.*

*Following the lead
of a woman has brought us
to this distress.*

Even Ailill insisted: *Good
is the wife of a good man.*

Reduced to anatomy,
she felt like a trout
cut on red sandstone.

Is it any wonder
she took up seduction
and the sword?

2

He left her
the hard choices.

Three enchanted monsters
in the shapes of cats.
Three men, competing,
of course.
        Who's best?

Conall and Laegaire
climb the rafters. Cuchulain,
as usual, strikes when provoked,
sits through the night, watching.

Who wins?

Ailill's voice slips
like a sword off stone:

danger in whatever judgement.

She's left holding
the bronze, silver, and gold.

   3

This much seems clear:
Maeve never thought the love
of a man alone could save her,

but Ailill released her from fear.
He loved her directly as daylight.

Together they built a house
of oak, fitted with bronze,
red yew carvings.

Flocks of white birds
might rise from the Hill of the Sidhe
withering all they touched,
enchanted pigs could trample
the earth barren.

But Ailill and Maeve shone
like bronze pillars,
struck and vibrating.

   4

They both understood desire
for a beautiful woman,

her skin soft as feathers,
her mouth the beginning
of the world.

When Angus Óg
described years of longing,
they felt their own pulses
beat like wings. A woman

in their district,
hair the color of sky
at dusk.

Who cares she was nothing
but trouble, under some fool
enchantment, one year herself,
the next a wren, herself again,
then pheasant or starling or sparrow.

Listening to Angus Óg's desire,
their hearts rose up like song.
Later they gave their bodies
to each other as if
they themselves might be more
than earthbound flesh.

And though some thought it
merely politic when Maeve and Ailill
forced the secret of her spell,
it was more impulse than plan.

They flew toward consummation,
flutter of tongue, hum of thigh.
Not themselves, they made
themselves utterly at home.

And Angus Óg became a swan,
which was, after all,
the variety of bird his beloved
had most recently become.

5

She was blamed for the weakness
of the men of Ulster

as if her strength
could only be stolen,
an easy theft, from men.

But their own cruelty
betrayed them.

When enemies closed in,
the men of Ulster felt
their arms refuse to lift swords.
Pain seared their bellies
and their legs trembled
as if they had been walking
for days.

They were cursed for forcing
a woman to outrun horses.
They had threatened her.
Her husband would die.

When she fell to the ground
and gave birth, the boy and girl
awash with blood, her cry pierced
the bodies of birds and lodged
in the ringed trunks of trees,

lodged in the throats
of the men themselves
who were suddenly spent.

Neither making life nor taking
life, they felt weak.
But Maeve had nothing to do with it.

6

Fergus was different.
He walked away from king and country
for love of a woman
he could not have.

Like a serpent swallowing
its own tail, Maeve asked him
for what would dissolve
armies and thrones
if every man gave it,

love beyond borders, the heart
opening to what it most needs,
another heart to change it.

When Ailill understood
that his wife's body
was not entirely his own,
he responded with tact,
even wit. Carving a sword
from oak, he slid it into Fergus'
sheath, lifted the real blade
from among scattered clothes.
The hilt caught in Maeve's
robe, and for a moment
Ailill felt the earth
tilt, an ache in his body
deeper than sleep.

7

She had never met a man
who neither feared nor desired her.

When he came to Connaught
with the men of Ulster,
the sound of their horses
was like thunder on the roof.

Dark, he wore crimson, a brooch
of inlaid gold. Over his shoulders
a shield rimmed in silver.

His confidence scoured her
like a loud wind in winter.
He had lain with women of the Sidhe.
He had never lost a battle.

She offered food, ale, vats
of cold water, a ready bed.
He looked through her
as if she were mist.

Later when Maeve sent armies
against him, and Cuchulain had killed
many men, she imagined kneeling
before him, her arms circling his thighs,
her mouth busy, his voice unharnessed
from its burden of strength,
wild and ungovernable.

   8

Didn't she speak to the eel
of every color? She dipped
the bronze cup into the river
and brought up the mauve head,
the saffron tail:

What way is it with you?

For a moment
she was only herself
in love with the world.
The story alone was enough:

Two swineherds transform into eels
and are drunk down by cows.
The cows give birth to bulls,
the white-horned and the Brown.

Men in the bellies of bulls.
Brilliant eels speaking.
The whole of life, enchanted,
before her

and she chose the game
of status.

What will happen to me
after I get the sway
over Connaught?

9

Here is the hardest thing:
to change the old ways
of living.

Knowing what she knew
about women reduced to flesh,
Maeve bartered her daughter
anyway: sixty black-grey horses
with golden bits and twelve milch cows
with red-eared calves.

She sat past dark
with her daughter's lover,
playing chess, her gold queen
catching the last of the light,
the young man's hands beautiful
against the white bronze of the chessboard.

His dark hair curled at his jaw.
They argued about the marriage portion.
When their eyes met, she felt
a chilled wave.

Candle flames lanced
emeralds and rubies.
The dinner hour lapsed

and she forgot husband and kingdom,
forgot her own daughter,
her body bolder than the future.

Was it her unkissed lips
that drew her to Ailill's plan?
When Fraech left her check-mated,
hungry, the silver pawns scattered,

she recalled the prophecy:
death by water the Druids said.
How unmeasured the desire
that led her to the bank
of that river, Fraech flailing,
water snakes thick in the current.

10

If only he hadn't begun
Good is the wife of a good man.

She might have chosen silence.

But when he said, *You are better
today than the day I married you,*

she saw a gored bull in the twilight.

*I was good before I ever
had to do with you*

and with that the great tally began,
how many horses, what price
the jewels, which robe finer,
her property set beside his,
as if a world that had wounded her
could finally settle her worth.

Even the white-horned bull,
calved in Maeve's herd, refused
to be owned by a woman, chose
Ailill's herds instead.

The war in the north came to this:
she went looking for a bull
better than his, though his bull
had once been hers.

A portrait of Maud Gonne by Sarah Purser, 1896

3. "Her Small Hands Were Not Beautiful"
Voices in the Act of Remembering Maud Gonne

Maud Gonne (1866-1953) lifelong [Irish] nationalist, was born in England.
—Caitriona Clear, *Encyclopedia of Irish History and Culture*

The poet W.B. Yeats fell in love with her, immortalizing her in verse.
—Margaret Ward, *Dictionary of National Biography, Missing Persons*

[Gonne's] devout faith centred on the 'holy trinity' of the people, the land, and the spirit of the nation.
—Karen Steele, *Maude Gonne's Irish Nationalist Writings, 1895-1946*

[W]ho can tell / which of her forms has shown her substance right?
—W. B. Yeats

Micheál MacLíammoír, the actor friend

    you can work it out
                        1917   I was only a boy
                                          I had expected
    a tall rose   I was confronted by
                               a black orchid
    she looked older than she was
                               unlike many beautiful women
    the bones of her face
                     imperishably beautiful   her eyes
    would have been so beautiful
                         if they hadn't had   this strange
    anger in them   like a tigress
                            golden eyes   golden hair   going grey
    deep black
                  whether for her husband
                                     whom she didn't love   or for Ireland
    I have never made up my mind

Francis Stuart, the son-in-law

    she always seemed to sail
                             into a room as I recall it
    in long black draperies
                           well I don't think I spoke much
                                             I was rather overawed
    and she had this manner   if you're critical you'd call it
                                                   effusive
    if you like it
                  you'd call it
                            outgoing   pretty un-Irish
    it was new to me
                      extraordinary activity
                                         ceaseless activity
    always something dramatic in the air
                                   she lived I think very much
    you know
                  in a state of semi-excitement
                                       it was *always, always, always*
    something of the greatest importance

Her Small Hands Were Not Beautiful

Imogen Stuart, the granddaughter-in-law

        this terribly tall and willowy woman
                                    those long limbs
    very old and dilapidated
                of course
                            I have never met
        anything before or after
                like her

Hilton Edwards, Micheál MacLíammoír's English lover

    a very gracious and charming lady
                            quite an amazing person
shall I say
            obsessed   a lady obsessed
                              there's no question
about that   but always
                very gracious
                            I've never found anything
any anti-English feeling
                personally
                        a great quality I've noticed
in all the Irish people
            I've met everybody
                            from politician to gunmen
sometimes both combined
                certainly never against me   personally

Seán McBride, the son

    she used to read me chunks of Irish history
                          we had a house at the seaside
        lots of friends
               from Ireland
                      a very happy cheerful
  kind of life

Louisa Coghlan O'Brien, the IRA secretary to Seán McBride

    so I wouldn't know
            when   I first met her   she was always there

if you know what I mean

...coming time can say,
'He shadowed in a glass,
What thing her beauty was.'

[Gonne's} father was an army officer and her mother died when she was five. The family then moved to Ireland, a country that Gonne adopted as her own.

—Clear

Imogen

    she was first and foremost   I think
                                          an eccentric
strongly pro-German
                  [during *both* World Wars]

    she wasn't interested in anybody
                              very much
                                          only herself
and her own thing   you know
                                  she loved her grandchildren
        but I don't think she took much personal interest
                                                        in anybody

Seán

          the assassination of the Archduke
                                      I remember mother being
very worried
               a trainload of dying and wounded arrived
        somebody who'd immediately organize a hospital there
                                              mother pretty well
    running it
                the wounded and dead
                              unloaded on the quays

Hilton

    I'm a very apolitical person
                                myself   keep off the subject
    I think I sang God Save the King
                            to her   on one occasion
    we were discussing   how foolish
                            to debase   national anthems
    usually a means of getting the audience
                                   out of the house
    singing them out
                  after every performance   I think it was MacLíammoír
    who pointed out
                  foolish of the Irish
                                  to follow suit
    one should save   the national anthem

    for a significant occasion
                          I found myself singing
    and suddenly   I thought
                      my god, I'm singing "God Save the King"
    to Maud Gonne MacBride
                         but   I must admit   she
    didn't bat an eyelid

Micheál

    always in black   I can't remember her

      in any other color   this cadaverous look about her

    this unexpectedly light voice
                        you know   she spoke like that

    very pleasant   the most beautiful manners
                                   I've ever known in any lady

She is foremost of those that I would hear praised.

Educated privately at home, Gonne was given an unusual amount of freedom at an early age.
        —Clear

Louisa

    They were terribly friendly
                              but they were
  not exactly on each other's
                        wave length   Madame Markeviecz
    was the militant type
                     and no soft stuff with her   Madame [Gonne] McBride

was so gentle   so thoughtful, so kind
                    they would both be ascendancy types
                                                and I tell you
  ascendancy types
              they don't treat each other   with any difference

only Irish peasant types
                  getting up off their knees
                                      as we all were
  would have any class feeling
              like that   or a necessity to
touch the cap   or anything like that
                                no, ridiculous

Seán

    she had a set income
                  investments   you know
                                  from her family

Colonel Gonne died in 1886 and on her twenty-first birthday Maud inherited a substantial income.
        —Ward

Francis

    unlike many mothers
                her vital interest was not
                                  the marriage of her daughter
            we went off without
her knowledge
            she certainly did disapprove
                          very much so

Her Small Hands Were Not Beautiful

    then we came back after a time
                          and got married
                                             and then of course
there was the black and tan war
                         in which we were all   engaged
I remember going round there
                  one day
                                  the place had been ransacked
by the troops   obscenities had been
                              scrawled
she accepted it
                the marriage   I don't say we ever got on very well
we had nothing
           in common whatsoever
                             but I never found any resentment

In 1887 [Gonne] went to France, where she published *L'Irlande Libre (Free Ireland)* and took part in the extreme [French] nationalist Boulangist movement along with her lover, Lucien Millevoye, with whom she had two children, Georges (1890-1891) and Iseult (1894-1954).
                                                —Clear

Francis

    I would call her rather   a one-tracked mind
                                            but not petty
she wasn't a petty woman
                       she had breadth
emotionally quite a breadth
                           she read articles constantly   and newspapers
she must have read at one time
                            quite a lot of French novels
she listened to a lot of music
                       loved Wagner   a lot of other music
she wasn't intellectual
                her world was neither the world
                                             of the artist
nor less of the scientist
                    it was a world   I would say
                                        of the emotionally
committed   she had people around her
                               fanatically committed to groups

     somewhat frustrated
                    this was a sort of compensation
                                      a sexual emotional coldness
extraordinary
               the feeling I got   of extraordinary lack
emotional
               sensual lack   I suppose that is fairly obvious
                                        older men
her relationship was largely other   than sexual
                                being
I mean   being sexual in one case
                      or two

They were unable to marry (Millevoye, a Roman Catholic, was separated from his wife) but their 'passionate alliance' against the British empire lasted fifteen years.
      —Ward

she cried into this ear / 'Strike me if I shriek.'

Micheál

    I didn't really know her well
                            until about the 1930s   she used to come and see us
    we had a flat in Dorset
                      I remember the way she loved
                                        a low chair
    every time she'd mention   England
                            she'd bash her fist
on the floor
               England lived definitely
                              in the coal cellar   Ireland
lived somewhere in the roof   she'd say   *strike a blow for Ireland*
    and point this long hand
                           up at the ceiling

Hilton

    fanatical in her manners
                    in her whole attitude   but
                                    I'm not going to criticize
    obviously   it was very sincerely felt
                          somewhat extremely expressed

Back in Ireland in the 1890s, Gonne took part in the on-going land campaign, focusing media attention on hunger and poverty in Donegal. In 1900 she founded Inghínidhe na Héireann (Daughters of Ireland), a nationalist organization that concentrated on the teaching of the Irish language, support for Irish manufacturers, and anti-recruitment activities.
—Clear

Louisa

    I was 9 or 10

                      or something   when she came to live   I'm not quite sure

she was only on the periphery

                        of my life   no personal contact with her

at all   *come in and say hello*   *how do you do and Madam's here and so*

Madam had a shell card industry

                                I'm sure you've heard of it

started off to help the poor people

                                women's husbands were in jail

needed some work

                so she must have run out

                                  of poor people to help

or something   anyhow   she asked my two sisters

    to come help her with it

                      I'll tell you one thing

Madam would have nothing to do

                            with the jam factory

           wouldn't have been her thing   she was artistic

                                            no jam

wouldn't have been her thing

1890   [Gonne] refused membership in Celtic Literary Society, National League, and Irish Republican Brotherhood (because of her gender).
—Steele

But O! twas bitter wrong
If he could pass her by
With an indifferent eye

Francis

    the black and tan war   especially

                                    it was really life and death struggle
between armed troops

                and the occupying power   a woman like Maud Gonne
bound to be

            on the periphery   and I should nearly think

rather in the way

                she did write a lot   and spoke a lot
I should imagine

            her value would have been   abroad

                                  America   France
but how far that was valuable   really

                            I don't know

Her United States lecture tour in 1897 raised the largest sums ever amassed for the [Amnesty Campaign], [which was dedicated to the release of political prisoners in England and Ireland as well as the support of their families].

                                                              —Steele

Francis

        my impression was

    the impact was far more   on the side of

                            helping   the families of prisoners
    meetings in O'Connell Street

                    every Sunday with her friend

                                  Madame Despard
on the question of prisoners   their conditions
and there I think she really did

                    have an impact   probably even was a thorn
in the side

        of the Free State   O'Connell Street had some ruins
they would

        speak   as I recall it

                    on these ruins   opposite the Post Office
both of them

        a great many

              working class women   sons or husbands
perhaps in prison

        or underground   would attend

                        Mrs. Despard rather strained

    very placid   had the money which Maud Gonne
                                              didn't really have
  very left wing whereas
                        Maud Gonne wasn't

1897 [Gonne] gives first public open-air speech at socialist meeting organized by [James] Connolly in Dublin.
                        —Steele

Though she had young men's praise and old men's blame,
Among the poor both old and young gave her praise.

Micheál

    Mrs. Despard
                agreed with Maud Gonne in political matters
    did a lot of work with her
                          speeches   certain things   they were known
    in what we called
                Dirty Dublin   the lowest spheres
                                        of Dublin society
  as Maud Gonne Mad
                  and Mrs. Desperate

Francis

    Maud Gonne wasn't
                you see   in my judgement
    Maud Gonne was not at all   to the left
                          she was a right wing nationalist
  with Millevoye and the Boulangusts
                    purely right wing
                                      her admiration for Hitler
  right wing   Yeats
               insofar as Yeats had any outlook
                                  well I don't think
  she had any for its own sake
                    any interest in Fascism

Human, superhuman, a bird's round eye

Micheál

    she was an extraordinary creature

        always reminded me of that terrible line of Yeats'
about the whole sex

    probably unfair to them   if one can be unfair to them

when one gives an idea to a woman she will turn it into a stone

    he filled her with

        a romantic love for Ireland   she thought of nothing else
she was

    the most complete fanatic

        I have ever met   [she'd say]
Willie was so silly

    absurdly exaggerating   *I was very pretty*   *you know*

always got my clothes in Paris

    the average Irish revolutionary woman is so

dowdy   *so bad for the cause*

    I reproached myself for not

patronizing Irish industries   *at the same time*

    better to look as well as one could

so I got my clothes   *in Paris*

    then my dear son

    was born thereabout

her mind used to wander a bit

In 1903 Gonne married John MacBride, who had fought with the Boers against the British. Their only child, Seán, was born in 1904, and a year later, they were acrimoniously divorced.
    —Clear

It's certain that fine women eat
A crazy salad with their meat.

Seán

    my mother gave me long talks

        afterwards about my father

    it was all praising him   you know

Micheál

                             she had one fabulous story   nobody will believe   *Could you, could you*   *find that letter from Mr. Oscar Wilde*
               thanking me for trying to rescue him   *from prison I don't know if you know*
                  Mr. Wilde   *who after all was the son of Speranza*   *why should he*
                          languish in an English jail?
why   *why*   *why*   she hit the floor
      came out with a most elaborate
                         sort of Monte Cristo escape story
files put into loaves of bread   and then
       they would row him down the river
                          get him into a boat cross the Channel   to France
                 Willie inspired her   asking her to sign a petition
      saying   "innocent"   "wrongly accused" *Willie, Mr. Wilde is not innocent*
                 but I will sign   *a blow against England why should he languish in an English jail?*
                      it did no good   they took not the faintest notice   the plan was
                to row him down the river
and Yeats said in a boat
               with painted oars   and I said   *Willie, we must be practical*
      and so when I wrote this story
                about Maud Gonne   I took it to her *ah, you're far too sweet about me*
            like Willie   *you exaggerate but dear Micheál*
        that story about poor Mr. Wilde   *complete and absolute fable*   *you must have dreamed it*   *I never*

1908   Gonne's mystical marriage to Yeats resumes. They become lovers briefly.
                                                                     —Steele

I might have thrown poor words away
And been content to live

Imogen

    he was just another dearie
                                  one of those dearies she had

Micheál

    she was very wonderful
                      really   I don't mean
  intellectually wonderful   her brain stopped too short   too suddenly
      far too romantic
                  to be a great intellectual   her interest in what she called
    the occult
           she nearly got mixed up
                              with Alistair Crowley
      you know   the black magician

Thereafter, Gonne divided her time between her house in Normandy, where Seán was mainly reared, and Ireland, where she continued to campaign politically, presiding over the foundation of Inghinidhe na Heireann's newspaper, *Bean na hÉireann* (*Woman of Ireland*) in 1908.
                            —Clear

Francis

    the one
        to me really human trait
                      was her fondness for cooking

Micheál

            she was blissfully indifferent
                            to anything she ate or drank
  or anything
        at all   except clothes   full of a rather worn majesty
  her clothes were well-worn
                French   exquisite material   exquisitely cut

        gold ornaments on her hair
                              looked the part of the life   always

Imogen

            I don't think she had any sense of humor
                                        in fact
    she was a most talented person
                          could act
                                could paint
                                        could draw
           she did the most beautiful flowers
                              so much style
    such wide interests
                a renaissance person

Micheál

          a grand romantic dottiness

    she'd say wonderful things   *hunger is the most sacred thing of the world*

hunger for freedom
                  she believed there was such a thing as freedom
which fascinated me because I don't, you see   maybe in heaven

the first thing normal people do
                          heterosexuals do   if they're really in love
is to bind themselves by bonds
                        the instinct to bind oneself to things
she wasn't free   she was sworn to Irish freedom   she was no more free
      than anything   than that wretched cat   you know

Hilton

Micheál and I
            are so well rehearsed   whatever differentiations
in the truth of our versions
                we reconciled these
                              into a consolidated front
by now   ha ha
              by sheer rehearsal   our versions are now agreed

Micheál

            I don't know whether   she would be too tall
to be an actress
                Sarah Bernhardt   she told me
                                                  encouraged her
  I don't think she was lying
                  I don't think she was a liar at all
  I heard her mention Iseult   yes
                                with great affection
and Sean   when I said
                      wasn't she proud of him   or something
she said   *he must go his own way*
                                we all do in the end
no   she was strange   difficult
                            to describe her   so purely a figure
of romance   stepped out of "Wind Among the Reeds"

She looked in my heart one day
And saw your image was there

Francis

                         I wouldn't call her a passivist
                                       I don't think
she was one of those women who revelled
                        in violence
                                  she had nursed
the wounded in Paris
           during the war
                      I won't say it's an act now
                                    Why
would I?
    I mean
        she did do a certain amount of hovering
                                  around beds
of the wounded
      in her house
            I don't think she could do much   but
she did what she could

Her Small Hands Were Not Beautiful

1918   Escapes to Ireland in disguise (January).... Arrested on 19 May on suspicion of being party to a pro-German plot.
—Steele

In 1918 she spent time in Holloway Gaol with Constance Markievicz and Kathleen Clarke; she was also imprisoned during the Civil War of 1922 to 1923, in which she took the Republican (anti-treaty) side.
—Clear

the minds that I have loved,
The sort of beauty that I have approved,
Prosper but little

Seán

                                                           she had to promise she wouldn't go
to Dublin
                and they wouldn't even say she could go back to Paris
she was bent
            on getting back to Ireland
                                and then mother got to taking
Turkish baths for her rheumatism again
                              you see
                                        and they're very long
so she was taking a Turkish bath
                        —Square
                                          some place
around there
            and they naturally got to know that Turkish baths
lasted
        for about three hours   three or four hours
                                              and they'd go
have a drink in the meanwhile   you know
                                  and my job was I watched
the Scotland Yard man
                    I would wake up and make my way
to where the Turkish baths were
                          watch the Scotland Yard man
going off to the apartment
                  usually about two hours
                                      and so finally
when D-Day came
                she came out of the Turkish bath   15 minutes

    after she'd gone in
                              Patricia and I went up to Sylvia's house
  in the old fort wall
                in the east end of London
                                        and there she was duly
disguised and all that
                   as a very old woman
                                      bent up
white hair and very bent up
                          she was perfectly easy to disguise
she went from London
                  by Liverpool   or some odd way
                                           and then
  she came here
                she was arrested
                                sent to Holloway
Josephine was in London with me then
                            in Woburn Place
                                          and she used to
  cook dishes   and bring them over
                                to Holloway Jail

Louisa

  I went to work
                as Seán's secretary
                                for the IRA
she was still active in what we call
                            the movement
I mean   she was going her way about it
                                  not in the IRA   as such
but because of Seán   she would always know
                                    what was going on
all that kind of thing
                    and Madam made speeches   every Sunday morning
you know
                she'd go to O'Connell Street
                                  herself and Mrs. Despard
and make speeches
                    she did it all the time   on behalf of the prisoners
there were still political prisoners   up to 1932 when DeValera got in

Her Small Hands Were Not Beautiful   47

    she was against DeValera

                      she was for DeValera   no, I'd have to give a lot
of thought
         to what her feelings were

1922   Gonne joins Peace Committee, converts home to makeshift hospital for injured Republicans and helps establish Women's Prisoners' Defense League, serving as Secretary.
                —Steele

Francis

    she never got up

           mornings

                    I'm speaking now of Roebuck house

                                where
    she was already an old woman

                she only got up

                      at lunch

                             I remember
    going to her room with Iseult

                and she would have a bottle

                            of white wine
    she would be in bed reading

            articles

                    or writing   the canaries
    would be chattering

           singing

As though a sterner eye looked through her eye

Louisa

    my recollection of her in those days

                          she was in bed
    she never got up

           very early   but she scribbled away

                                she was always
    writing   and Anna her grandchild

                  I'd never seen her pay much attention

    to children before
                        but she adored Anna
                                        and Anna was always
    running in and out
                      coming up and that
                                    and Madame was always there
    writing   I've never seen her in that she wasn't
                                      writing
    she would lie there   writing, writing, writing
    and an awful lot of people
                     thought she was dead   when she needed people
    when she was lying in bed
                     Hilton and Micheál   they were so good to her
    you know
                just coming and sitting and talking
                                    with an old lady in bed

Hilton

    she knew that Micheál
                    was an Irish scholar
                               writer of Irish
                                      lover of Irish
    lover of Irish things   I think she accepted me more
                                    because I was a friend
    I cannot claim
                myself   to have made any effort   specifically
    for Ireland
                I'm a professional   happened to be here
    I hope it's good
                for the town and the country   I would be sailing under
    mostly false colours
                if I said I did   though I think Micheál   one the other hand
    had this purpose
                    she recognized   I was assisting him
    rather than
                retarding him   she let a little bit   [of] the tar from the brush hand
    rub off on me   I was grateful

Micheál

    she was disappointed in Yeats   I think
                          because he wouldn't
                                      he couldn't
God help him   unnatural basis
                        for a man passionately in love
    physically in love
                with a woman   to be offered friendship instead of
you know   somebody looking for Michealangelo   given a stone marker
        Willie only interested me in his poetry when it was about Ireland
she couldn't accept his love poems
                      the awful thing she said
  you see, Willie could have done so much more for Ireland
                                      Yeats suffered deeply
        he was miserable about her

Many people know of Gonne only as the inspiration for some of W. B. Yeats's finest love poems, but though she was fond of "poor Willie," as she called him, she played a much greater part in his life than he did in hers.
                                                                                            —Clear

O she had not these ways
When all the wild summer was in her gaze

Seán

        Yeats
                she was fond of him
                                  she had a great respect for him
    as a writer   a poet
                      contempt for his political viewpoints
        she thought he was looking for too many honors
                                      a snob   yes
      who cowtowed
                  who liked cowtowing to British aristocracy
he was being ruined
            by too much flattery   in England

The execution of John MacBride after the 1916 Rising elevated Gonne's nationalist status as a 1916 widow and enabled her to return to Ireland with Seán.
      —Clear

Francis

                        yes, always, always   the widow's veil, black
it seems to me
                      wound round   forehead to back
                                                            she said it was
her uniform

Louisa

Seán doesn't laugh   so much
                                but then he's on a different plane
you know   very few traits in common
                              except for one   they believed
their own propaganda
                      if that means anything to you   Madame
never tried to be accepted
                      by anybody
                                  self taught   she hadn't got much
formal education
                but very well-read
                          from her time in Paris and with Yeats
and all these types   but her formal education   practically *nil* I'd think
      when she wasn't writing
                          she was reading Irish history and James Connolly
and all that

Seán

I got myself tangled up in the IRA and things
                                                she was afraid for me
you know   she was always worrying
   something would happen to me   you see

Her Small Hands Were Not Beautiful

        I remember being in Donegal
                                    impressed and frightened
at the devotion of the people
                    you walk into a house
                                      and people kneel
        down and kiss her dress   and so on

Or else I thought her supernatural

Micheál

    she loved to travel with caged birds
                            let them out on the night before the election
all that symbolism
                a romantic fanatic   a very beautiful one
like so many   not only fanatical people   Winston Churchill   Padraic Pearse
        half-blood
                half blood of the enemy   Maud Gonne was half English

Louisa

    she had this monkey
                hated everybody but herself
                                  stand on your hair
she was always talking about   I couldn't have made the name up   Dagda
    and there was a cat called   some Irish word
                                always talking about her father
Tommy she called him   her separations from him and ill treatment
    from the aunts   I don't think it scarred her in the end
    but she suffered
                it was a political marriage
                                    regret
is too big a word
            because she'd have Sean as a result
                  she was never going to love anybody
except the Millevoye man
              she had a horror of drink   I think this was a result

of MacBride's
                               she wouldn't say much against him   except this
she would refer to this
                     horror of drinking   oddly enough
                                         for a woman who has
a reputation
            a dark class woman   she wasn't
                             she didn't seem to have any interest
in sentimental attachments to men
                     whatever you know
I couldn't do without male company
    there's so many women in Ireland   you know   all unattached
    and you find yourself
                    going around in a herd of women   I don't care for it
I mean
         I must have the cut and thrust
                         of the male mind

Micheál

what Yeats said
               in one of his poems
that her small hands were not beautiful
                             she had beautiful hands
small   nervous
            quite beautiful hands   with those awful brown patches
that I'm getting now
            beautifully shaped hands
                        I thought
                                he thought
more of her beauty
        I imagine   than I would have done   I only knew
    one photograph
             the period of her great beauty   the nineties
the first years
      of this century   she was more boldness and passion and temperament
than any of those
          actual great beauties
                     the other pictures   all spoiled

Her Small Hands Were Not Beautiful

    I admit   by beribboned and befeathered hats
           a very, very pretty woman
                         I couldn't quite see
  this greatest beauty since Helen

Imogen

    I always thought Iseult
                much more beautiful

Sarah Purser's portrait of the young Maud is in the National Gallery of Ireland and a bust of her by Lawrence Campbell stands in the Hugh Lane Gallery. Neither does justice to her extraordinary beauty.
                —Ward

But one man loved the pilgrim soul in you,
And loved the sorrows of your changing face.

Francis

    she had a peculiar   rather haggard
    type of figure   and face
                      very strange eyes   you know
  not strange
        but memorable
                    the pupil   the golden pupil
  you looked into her eyes
        you never forgot them

Seán

    she used to laugh quite a bit
                    but not a great deal   you know
        rather serious
              and rather happy
                      she worked terribly hard always
      she'd get angry
           with traitors
                  Arthur Lynch made his peace
    with the British
        he came to the house in the British uniform
    and she just let fly

Micheál

    I heard her at the corner

    off of O'Connell Street

                          mounted on a wagon   on a pile of sugar boxes

fellow rebels!

              the Russians have the Czar under lock and key

                                     and I wish to God

we had our own King George

                          in the same place

                                     and off she was taken

    by the British police

A Helen of social welfare dream
Climb on a wagonette to scream.

Seán

    she was closely involved

        with the celebration of '98

                          I know this because everyplace I go

      not now so much

               as 20 years ago

    this old man comes up to me

        oh Seán   there's the day your mother

                                    unveiled the statue

Louisa

    I was only a little girlie around the place

                          she was dying   took her a long time to die

      she wasn't able to get up   at all   for a long, long time   a year

    you know

        she broke her arm or her hip   went into hospital   she got

    pneumonia

    and she didn't want to get better

                      she wanted to die then

and they said no
                    they couldn't let her die   they had new drugs
the world's greatest beauty
    now she was nothing   we used to talk about this
                                                            naturally
I was never beautiful
                    how can you take it   you've had the whole world
   at your feet   there she was   lying in bed
people thought she was dead   I used to sit with her quite a lot
            especially towards the end   I don't remember all that much
because it was so sad   so emotional
                                              she used to talk about Willie
    the early days   the shenanigans they used to be up to
taking these drugs and all that   they tried everything you know
    in the way of excitement
                                    she'd tell me this thing about
leaving her body   you know   she was full of that stuff
    not drugs or anything   she gave that up   very quickly
            she was afraid   she really became afraid
                                                induced to leave their bodies
and she'd look at it   it might not want to come back
            going around up there   forever
she was terribly fond of him
            she'd smile and say   *poor Willie*   but she never loved anybody
    except this Millevoye   she never did love
anyone else   she had these three children   two   the one that died
when I'm in the coffin   she says   *over in the drawer*
go over and put your hand in   and take out a little pair of booties
 and put those   in the coffin   with me
don't tell
            don't let anyone else know   I had great trouble
getting them into the coffin   without anybody knowing

And I that have not your faith, how shall I know
That in the blinding light beyond the grave
We'll find so good a thing as that we have lost?

Seán

    she was quite religious   you know

                                        very impressed with

St. Francis of Assisi

                    we spent about a week

                                      in Assisi

her father

                she talked about him a lot

and he would treat her as a grown-up

                              saying to her   *never be afraid*

        that created a bond   between them

                            but she was always telling me

she talked about him quite often

                          telling me so & so

so & so   so & so

Micheál

    an over-tall woman as a rule   is an embarrassment

to herself as to all

                    and then to the world   Maud Gonne was the only

        very tall woman   I've ever known

                                who loved her height

    she revelled in it   Yeats did too

Louisa

    there'd be no reason of my having   anything of hers

    she was never all that nice to me

                            she was a very benevolent woman

so kind

        I don't remember her

                    ever saying anything against anybody

unless it was DeValera and the sort

                        I never heard her   personally

be cross or nasty about anybody

maybe I'm wrong   I don't know   maybe since time's gone this far

I can't remember it

Micheál

 her description of meeting Wilde

he said I looked like a water lily

          in the letter he wrote from prison

              thanking me   he said

your suggestion is

       most romantic   most kind

            but I feel too depressed

in body and mind

to undertake such strenuous exercise

        as your adventure seems to me to suggest

it was all that way   with her

      it was all   so emotional

she was quite

    quite wonderful

         Markeviecz   didn't seem to mind dirt

smells   the reality of poverty

       would have distressed Maud Gonne

she was of

    a more delicately aesthetic balance   aesthetic nature

her mistake

    if she made a mistake   she was meant   really

to be an artist

Seán

oh my mother and my wife got along

         absolutely   they took to each other

 the whole time

    old age   she accepted it

        that was that   you know

and there's nothing you can do about it

       right up to her death

          she was very

careful about her appearance

     terribly keen on gardening

          pets in the house

 always   the birds used to sing

     lots of canaries   and dogs

and ordinary household things   like cooking

    you know   she was an excellent cook

        she used to really enjoy that
                                  put in quite a lot of work at it
  most of her friends were political as well   political and personal
              she was very fond of Connolly
                                James Connolly   you know
    had a big influence on her
                         I think she didn't like
                                          Lady Gregory
particularly
            she liked Con[stance]
                          but she didn't think much of her pictures

Maud Gonne hated being a 'prisoner of old age.'
                                    —Ward

old bellows full of angry wind

Louisa

   if you have to think about if another person
                         laughs or not   it must mean   they possibly didn't
   there was never any upstage stuff
                                on her part   but she had this regal bearing

Micheál

   she'd throw her head back
                       and laugh   I can't remember
   at what   but I remember her laughing

Francis

   I would never complain
   about her   she treated me with   mostly
                                       in many cases   with
   kindness
     she was interested
                      in gardening
                                 in collections of plants

                               in miniature Japanese trees
                                                a collection of birds
                                                                   I rather think people
            certainly in my case   who keep pets
                                                    make a certain fuss over them
                    they don't have close relationships
                                                with other human beings

Louisa

   now Madame was funny actually
                 the only person I heard her say anything against   was Stuart
   when the second child was born   she berated Stuart
          for saddling Iseult   with another child   it was so *unlike*
   Madam
                     so unlike her   she adored Iseult
                                                       possibly she was sorry
   about the whole thing   for Iseult's sake   you know
   if anything touched on Iseult
                                       she'd get very cross

Micheál

   you see
               her own lovely book
                           Servant of the Queen   the astonishing statement
   of a charming child
                              she found in Paris   called Iseult   a very sweet
   dedication   to *Micheál MacLiammóir*
                                                        *for all he had done
   and his great work*   *for Ireland*
                                     that had to come in
   I who was mad about the 1890s   *oh yes, poor poor Aubrey Beardsley
         such a delicate boy   such a talent*
                                              but she wasn't really interested
   back to Ireland
                       before you could say *knifed*   you know

Louisa

  Iseult was a strange person
           she suffered from being illegitimate
 and they hid it for a long time
         saving Iseult saving Sean
 because they said terrible things
          about Madame you know
  in Irish politics horrible names
            they put stories around
 she was just a prostitute
         one man in her life and she was so faithful to him
 but she was always leaving him
        coming to Ireland to work for Ireland and just
  leaving him

They have spoken against you everywhere,
But weigh this song with the great and their pride;
I made it out of a mouthful of air,
Their children's children shall say they have lied.

Micheál

  I came up with floods of Irish *how wonderful*
  he's talking Irish she didn't think it was as important
                as I did
   political freedom as she called it
         was everything
               she said
 Micheál dear talk about the beauty of old age
            don't believe a word of it
 it's hell
       endlessly wonderful
           she was very fond of Hilton
 he's so sympathetic *he's so charming*
          I keep forgetting
 he's an Englishman

Hilton

  I have to repeat the word

>   obsession
>   knowing her particular   obsession
>   her great courtesy and kindness
>   to me
>   because I wouldn't have been at all surprised
>   a person thinking as she does
>   like she did
>   so extremely   had been a little
>   frigid towards me
>   but   there was no question of this
>   in fact   it was markedly
>   the other way

All that sternness amid charm
All that sweetness amid strength

Louisa

>   she was deeply religious   very deeply religious   her conversion
>   to Catholicism was a big thing in her life   it went against everything
>   that was happening all around her   with her own people
>   very religious
>   very emotional   when I think of her
>   and her dying   it was the first time   anything like that had happened to me
>   I shook for days
>   the priests were there
>   and I was sitting with her when she
>   I'd never seen anybody die before

Gonne died at Roebuck House, her Dublin home, 27 April 1953, surrounded by her family.
            —Ward

Why, what could she have done, being what she is?

Micheál

>   I honestly don't feel there's much more
>   I can tell you

Glossary

In July of 1973, Irish studies scholar Conrad Balliet interviewed a number of Maud Gonne's family members, friends, and acquaintances. The largely unpublished transcripts of these interviews now reside in the Manuscript, Archives, and Rare Book Library of Emory University in Atlanta, Georgia. The poem "Her Small Hands Are Not Beautiful" has been found in the interviews as a sculpture might be found in an intriguing piece of granite. Most words and phrases appear in the poem in the same order as they appeared in the interviews. Each speaker is indicated by name at the first appearance and by his or her relationship to Gonne; through compression, selection, interleaving, and the physical arrangement of lines on the page, the poem distills my sense of the speakers' feelings about Gonne. I have also included commentaries by historians and other scholars as well as quotations from W. B. Yeats's poems. Finally, mine is only one poet's interpretive, impressionistic act. Many more readings are possible.

Speakers in the Poem

Micheál MacLíammoír, Gonne's actor friend: Born in London in 1899, Alfred Willmore reinvented himself as a Cork native, adopting an Irish name with the persona, and working as a prominent actor in the Irish theater for 50 years, where he acted in over 300 roles. With his life partner, Hilton Edwards, he founded the Gate Theatre in Dublin in 1928, and he also cofounded the Irish-language theater, An Taibhdhearc, in Galway. He was the author of 13 plays, and he appeared in many films and television drama. At the time of his interview with Balliett, MacLíammoír was 74 years old. He died four years later, in 1978.

Hilton Edwards, another of Gonne's actor friends: Micheál MacLíammoír's lover and life partner, Edwards was born in London in 1903. Settling in Dublin, he was an influential actor, director, and producer, and along with MacLíammoír, he founded the Gate Theatre imn Dublin in 1928. He directed MacLíammoír in the role that made him internationally famous, that of Oscar Wilde in *The Importance of Being Oscar*. Edwards was 70 at the time of his interview with Balliett.

Glossary

Francis Stuart, Gonne's son-in-law: Married to Gonne's daughter, Iseult, between 1919 and 1939, Stuart was a novelist born to Ulster Protestant emigrants in Australia in 1902. After the early death of his father, his mother returned with him to Ireland. He was the author of 20 novels, most famously *Black List Section H* (1971), and he became a controversial figure because of his involvement in the 1930s with the Nazis. Stuart was 71 when Balliet interviewed him, and he lived for 97 years, dying in 2000.

Imogen Stuart, Gonne's granddaughter-in-law: Born in Berlin in 1927, Stuart married Francis and Iseult's son, Ian, in 1951 and moved to Ireland where she is now well-known as a sculptor. Her work in stone, wood, and metal can be found in many public spaces across Ireland, especially in churches. She currently resides in Dublin, and she was interviewed by Balliet when she was 46.

Seán McBride, Gonne's son: Born in France in 1904, MacBride remained in France until his father's execution by the English after the Easter Rising of 1916. He returned to Ireland with Maud Gonne MacBride at twelve and joined the IRA during the 1919-21 War. During his lifetime, he was a Chief of Staff for the IRA, an Irish government minister, and a prominent international figure. Continuing his mother's work for political prisoners, he was a leader in Amnesty International; he received the Nobel Peace Prize in 1974 and the Lenin Peace Prize in 1977. He was 69 when Balliet interviewed him.

Louisa Coghlan O'Brien, a family friend and the IRA secretary to Seán McBride (No photo available)

A Note on the Author

Raised in the nomadic subculture of the U.S. military, Kathryn Kirkpatrick was born in Columbia, South Carolina, and grew up in the Phillipines, Germany, Texas and the Carolinas. Today she lives with her partner, Will, and their two shelties in the Blue Ridge Mountains of North Carolina, and she currently holds a dual appointment at Appalachian State University as a Professor in the English Department and the Sustainable Development Department. She has a Ph.D. in Interdisciplinary Studies from Emory University, where she received an Academy of American Poets poetry prize. Her poetry collections include *The Body's Horizon* (1996), selected by Alicia Ostriker for the Brockman-Campbell award; *Beyond Reason* (2004), awarded the Roanoke-Chowan Poetry Prize by the North Carolina Literary and Historical Association; *Out of the Garden* (2007), a finalist for the Southern Independent Booksellers Association poetry award; *Unaccountable Weather* (2011); and *Our Held Animal Breath* (2012), selected by Chard DeNoird for the Brockman-Campbell award. As a literary scholar in Irish studies and the environmental humanities, she has published essays on colonialism, post-colonialism, class trauma, eco-feminist poetics, and animal studies. Her edited collection, *Border Crossings: Irish Women Writers and National Identities,* was published by the University of Alabama Press in 2000.

www.ingramcontent.com/pod-product-compliance
Lightning Source LLC
Chambersburg PA
CBHW031127160426
43192CB00008B/1132